T0077479

catalien

Dryad Press (Pty) Ltd
Postnet Suite 281, Private Bag X16,
Constantia, 7848, Cape Town, South Africa
www.dryadpress.co.za
business@dryadpress.co.za

Cover design and typography: Stephen Symons
Editor: Michèle Betty
Copy Editor: Helena Janisch

Set in 9.5/14pt Palatino Linotype
Printed and bound by Digital Action (Pty) Ltd

First published in Cape Town by Dryad Press (Pty) Ltd, 2020
ISBN 978-0-6398091-5-1

catalien

Poems by
Oliver Findlay Price

DRYAD PRESS

People! Read Poetry

for
Hugh and Julia

CONTENTS

The soul unto itself
Is an imperial friend –
Or the most agonizing Spy
An enemy could send.

– Emily Dickinson, 'The soul unto itself'

Not, I'll not, carrion comfort, Despair, not feast on thee;
Not untwist – slack they may be – these last strands of man
In me ór, most weary, cry I can no more. *I can;*

– Gerard Manley Hopkins, 'Carrion Comfort'

A man cannot live without a steady faith in something indestructible
within him, though both the faith and the indestructible thing may
remain permanently concealed from him…

– Franz Kafka, 'Aphorism 50'

Alien

The child wails next door
in conversation with its coughing,
while the shrike cleans himself
and feeds on bread.
I am lord of the loaf,
indifferent as God
but as present as my thoughts.

I rest in my uniquity
without guilt or stress
and sprinkle kindness.
I cannot dream the killing of the bull –
the crowd's Dionysian roar,
its tearing flesh and drinking blood.
I am alien in this world.

I drop with the fall of a leaf,
dead of the drought,
lie in the must of the sand,
creep into the bellies of the sun-glassed ones,
their *sol y sombra,* their haired notches
acting their lust for the wilderness,
slender grooves tarnished,
milk blooded.

I judge without aquittal or sentence,
and help a spider from my water glass.

The cat at the loom

stitches a stroll in the garden,
a paused foot on moss,
torrent of golden Venusian hair,
merriment of dance and twitching skirt,
meander of rivulets,
its destiny a lake
where fish and cormorants leap and plunge.

The robin searches for segmented sweets
among the crumbs spilt by the affluent table.

An extravagant breeze
lifts misted veils,
disrobes trunks,
ascends to tufted canopies
where peacocks roost,
and, silent among the treetops,
charities of ageing ladies in floral blues
touch lips.

Academy Cat

He licks butter and laps water at the sink,
sprays the lattice outside to sign himself,
tiptoes through ceramic cattle
and the Oberammergau Marie on the *jonkmanskas*.

Sits in the curl of his tail,
pays disinterested attention to the weavers
who squabble for crumbs – and then –
mystic, wonderful, he pads

campus corridors, a theatre where the cat deity,
Bastet, markets the rules of war and creation.
Twitches his tail at the pigeon roost,
and takes his place.

Paws poised over paper and pen,
he bares his teeth and wrinkles his lip
at sparrows nestled in the hair
of the goddess.

He lids his eyes from the flash
of hers as she preaches academia's
stalk and catch without disturbance
to the make-believe forest.

Next, among the sprayers,
he kisses the finger of the gelded god
who soaks the reams of writing with the flat beer
of peer-reviewed citations and cash rewards.

Back at his digs, his canary room-mate
has fled – he is now an elite and subtle predator –
divinity and mummy-bandages
await him after death.

Territorial Cat

Landlord of seven erven,
all inhabited: four by humans,
one by a Dalmatian sheepdog
where I trespass during her sleep,
the rest by two passing feral cats
whom I see off with fearsome efficiency,
a grey mongoose who claims right of way
(which I tolerate diplomatically),
then lizards and mice who
pay rental with their lives.

Birds I leave alone – I know
my limitations – a flutter of wings is poor reward,
a mouthful of feathers no reward at all.

I roll on my back for Jack, the border collie,
then slip home through my private gate
for supper of tinned sardines
before a night on the stars.

In Tomcat's Dream

Beyond the house, the crashing surf,
and the grey leaf tree,
I live again night's fight,
our yowl and screech.

I twitch my tail at my name's sound,
dream pilchards in the blue-ring bowl,
my master's knuckled *Eisbein*
spans the double dish.

She's black, flashes scarf of white,
I know her in the dark –
brush my stripes and whisk my tail
to lure her amber eye.

She's reconciled to arse, I see,
hind-foot stretched to heaven –
cleans it with a nibble and lick.

Little human infant on his straw –
no vestigial vertebrae betray
the grave mistake:

you, rated higher
in a 'fundamental' sense, than
the butterfly that filters through my sleep.

Royal Bantam Priestess

Chainsaw my skull's round,
place a dish for rain and dipping beaks –
expose my yolk, an orange in my head.

One giant skip for a hen-keeper's daughter.

Take courage –
termites in their red iron towers,
multitudes, soft queens needing feeding –
and remember –

in my hands the snap from life to death,
a pluck and slit from anus to eggs,
my reading of the giblets – our salvation –
arms raised, white ants sigh,

and I am ordained.

A cat night-dances on the table
that lifts its foot and taps –
a vagrant at the window.

The weavers are away to their wards
and are sitting their eggs.

The hidden cause of my efficient clause –
my numbered yoke at the wagon-shaft –
I devote my weight, ox-like.

A yellow weaver grabs and carries
a crumb to his sitting wife,
over bush-tops to the bobbing nests at the pool.

I scatter grain for the scutter and peck of my hen.

Apotheosised,
she nestles the children of dust
under her wings.

Brown queen

of my imperfections,
mole on my wrist, benign friend –
you prod me to listen to
the cat's cry of my conscience,

to read the calming
twitch of my cat's tail.
Or do I come trailing
clouds of glory?

And when I cling to the party mask,
you teach me: *walk away from it,*
leave all, say no more,
take a ship.

Mine, the skirl of a gull,
the gannet's plummet – his lost column of salt,
the longbow maker – his straw target,
the flowering leaf in autumn – its winter fall.

And when I ask, *why am I here?*
Is this an end, a closed road ahead?
you sit me on a dolphin
and glide me into the water-melon moonrise.

Static on a Pillar

Weavers flip in the feeder,
roofed, one bread crumb for each,
a pendulous justice,
moments of thrill and fright,
flights to dependent woven homes.

Starlings in denial of the drought,
wing-up diamonds
in a tapering flat-topped bath.

A black cat in a white dress shirt
stalks and ponders,
pauses in a triangle of sun
for a tongued groom to her
immaculate mottled hind leg.

Under the grey wattle,
a red segmented scorpion
tickles my fingertips
on his sandpit pulpit,
clippers readied,
tail-light arched overhead.

Mole

I lie ugly on his wrist, sly and malignant –
brown, flat hillock – too large to be ignored.

All mortal are we – mole and host.
If I syphon off his life, then mine goes too –
we co-conspirators look to survive a little longer
than the foolish norm
saddled on us by actuaries.

He shows me off – yes,
I peep from below his cuff,
as he handles his dinner cutlery,
to be spied by the woman beside him,
and quiver an arrow down her wine-swaddled spine.

Oh no, he laughs, *she'll never earn the scalpel –
too dear to me* – I play cat's throat to his caressing finger.
His brother fists him in the face – he's not good enough for them –
I crown him alien to his fingertips.

Not the totem of his tribe – he's tribeless –
I'll never be excised and mounted on a pole,
for in his depressions
he rubs his lamp,
draws magic from my feel.

We rejoice in our joined bodies –
a hunchback and his hunch,
lie curled – and in the
end, as I foreshadow,
crumble into ash.

In the motes of time

that float amid the surges of duty,
I stand on the fo'c'sle head
to watch the bow cleave the silken sea.
I saw a shoal of hammerheads peel off to each side
like a parting garment.
Another time, as we lay at anchor off Kobe,
two dolphins, knitting purl and plain,
weaving helixes about each other's bodies,
made love in the sea's soft surge and fall.
Then I remembered a pair
that plunged in coils together off the promenade at Nice,
and told me: *go back to your hourglass starting point,*
where you were born,
do your duty by tribe,
before the sand runs out.

Alien am I, of no space, no place –
all is mine:
the girl who shaves my face in the square mosaic bath –
our cool kimono dreams – senses
time's devastations.

Love Letter

You escape your mother's Methodism
in my Catholic fritillaries of lace and incense.

We fairy-tale the shadows of our selves,
and stand tall a moment.

Those years –
gardens, books and children –

I, the knobbed and warted toad,
coaxed you to stone.

Trailing shrouds of story, I wrapped you
in your web of spider queen.

But you unmanned me in my manic wildness,
drove me to your method's wilderness.

We, crippled,
disinterred our jewels –
shuttered.

Everything Is Miracle

I shrivel, a trodden snail
in night's ether,
ooze and curl,
stoned and stopped.

I follow and obey,
don't care – don't matter.
My matter – a long,
sagging, slow smile.

After rain, each leaf
holds a pearl, glistens with the sun's climb,
shrinks in sun's mother-kiss.

The weaver snatches bread
from the tossing feeder,
carries a crumb to its
shivering feathered young.

The spring morning opens in booming silence.

Blood Moon

Tonight I show you my nakedness –
you, my anchor, my friend, my lover.

Your shade treks my skin and covers me,
displays the rusted round of me
and, this once in a hundred years,
I glow unclothed in your dark.

Your microbes wake from their nightmare
for less than a spot in the time of the cosmos,
then go back to their cancerous work –
scalding you to blistered ash.

Benign bacteria cling to your membranes
with asters on their breath, carry banners
for your green and blue and brown.
Oh earth, of all your children,

am I the eldest? Thrown into space,
always facing you, swooning in bonded orbit,
while they, with one small step for a microbe,
one giant leap for microbia,

scout my back and tramp my dust.

Snow Lover

She had the finest down on upper lip
and dressed in swaddling polo-neck and scarves.
You only noticed hair from closest up
creep down her inner thighs and silk her calves.

Though hot, she craved a fireside and book,
her feet curled up, a woolly dog below,
for me just one, in welcome, careless look,
a sizzling pan, outside the hush of snow.

She backpacked pen and paper, strode in boots
and sought the winter trees so spare and gaunt,
to draw the knotted coils of forest roots –
her secret forest room became my haunt.

At noon's snow melt, she fled – and I lost gold.
But then – she went without becoming old.

The Crossing to the Tea House

A rubber-nosed cane
finds and prods the curb's groin –
a plastic bottle-top, a curl of migrant sand.

He steps, one hi-tech boot
obediently in sequence to the other,
into the traffic's pour.

Wiped and pistled to the sound of flush,
the choir boy's treble at its childish noon –
remembered at this crossing's hush.

Wrapped and zippered
for the tea house, distantly green-shaded,
his wisp of brow scowls over red-webbed eye.

He lifts a claw to the incorporeal face,
eyeless behind a beetle's shield where it
grinds its nippers, impatient for his bones.

Without a stumble, he proceeds,
finds the curb with his cane –
curved t-top to his hand.

Then the Victorian tea house, creaking in its boards and cushioned –
the loose leaf tea's metallic smoulder fogs his tongue
and scalds the cold blue iron of his eyes.

Ulterior Motion

Can anything be in worse taste
than the utilitarian porridge mix of piss and semen?
Evacution and pro-creation, one location!
Therefore, there never was a creator-god
and I am relieved of belief in that mock-worthy fantasy.

In deference to my divinity,
I seek cover in leaves
blessing in blindness.
I plant an orchid in my navel,
soothe my sight on a turquoise sea,
drink African coffee
and kiss the moonrise
sitting on the bog
with the sunset of Torquemada
at my rear.

Jeweled and painted cardboard characters
tread the matchbox make-believe,
eat elaborate tinsel meals
but never shit,
not even in the dark holes of their plots.

I make-believe I come from stars,
arseless and beautiful
and in my rubble soak-away
I plant jonquils.

Psychopath

When I'm defined by deep psychiatry,
they lay my glib and superficial charm
quite bare, my playful grandiosity.
With lies, I'm in denial that I do harm.

No less will I admit to doing wrong.
And as for grief at suffering I cause,
why, let me rather chant a little song –
my victims spoiled their lives, I purge their flaws.

But you, my sly and shallow-pated friends,
eat meat with callous and remorseless calm.
Your victims, just like mine, meet frightful ends.
You're in denial, like me, that you do harm.

I'm cunning and manipulative too –
and these are qualities I share with you.

Untidy Lives

Untidy as ever
are the car-tyre lizard's times.

No fly treks his sky
to dare its life on his sun-mottled
cement step battlement.

He ventures grubbing
into dead-leaf hollows
creeping in shadow –
doing his other sunless self –
over rough landscape.

He pauses like a monument
on a foreign stone
to reaffirm his, *who am I?*

Then later, splay-toed, degraded,
he comes home full-bellied
to his cement ledge,

to the furrowed cool of his imperfections –
his pale-hearted fridge,
his junketing washing-machine –
until another day warms his blood's oil.

Empty Shells

She should have died hereafter – not this soon,
riding high clouds in winter's storm,
leaving me the frosted comfort of the moon –
dead compensation for her emptied form.

This coffined roof, these shrouds of rain –
this thrashing of the branch's unborn leaf –
fling out the question, *why should I remain?*
while my black sobs raise squalls of grief.

Her cry for water through the storm-wind's weep –
her blood-spot hands – her yesterday's tomorrow,
her search for peace torments her sleep,
her demons shriek my guilt, denude my sorrow –

and empty shells ripple the sea's brown foam,
roll seaward-shoreward, welcoming me home.

The Kidney of Rhetoric

The normality of humanity
is a bloodied heart and
mathematic head.

Can humans be humane?
Adjective to a miscreant noun,
delicately nourished on slivered livers,

minced thigh stuffed in tubes of gut,
screaming butchered knees
and severed ligaments?

What a destiny!
To be normal.

Strange

this 'we': a question?
The only home I know is 'I' –
the indestructible.

I am the palace where I walk,
the sweetness of its cluttered rooms;
I toast its gracious prospects,
their open emptiness.

But down in the streets
I encounter fights –
dogs with missing legs
and amputated barks –
and then,

I creep deep between forest boles,
drink from grooves behind her knees,
tongue the padding of her soles,
foxholed in her cabin among trees –

my other home.

Sometimes at night

when madam tinnitus coils her long lament
and the surf settles in sleep,
you can hear our planet –
that other soft hush through space.

But soon,
the cats parade my deck,
upset the rain-water bucket –
drip the stairs where the rabble shores its grief
in freaking frenzy,
flick their togas,
scare the masses with talk of bankers' plots,
throw bones to decide which cities to sack and when,
Ionic or Doric columns of dust, Corinthian blooms of cloud,
pause while the ancestors void their huts,
and come to lead them to an orange bliss
of plastic wrappings and condom headgears.

Then the planet,
spherical after all,
turns a little to let the sun
steep its valley rock and hill
in the true down duvet of warm
inevitable death.

The mask

flashes its eyelids to hoard esteem before it slips.
Feet scurry in the waiting room,
this way and that on the Oregon floor –
the suburban house re-appointed as doctors' rooms,
each chair weeping into the floor,
the hiss of black coals,
sighs hinting estuaries
and random triggers of plovers.
The bladder-headed man knows
a bird's habit if you name it,
clothes its eggs in sacramental theft.
Closeted, the wet metallic starfish guided
by two arms, an eyeless head,
explores spine, ribs and the hale of slack bags.
The absence of vestigial caudal vertebrae
signals evolutionary aristocratism.
The patient pallet groans with the floorboards.
The secretary sniffs into her telephone,
haunch-shouldered like a drinking cat.
Unmasked bones bottle-neck doorways,
curtsey, offer a seat to the crippled bi-pedal,
reduced to a solo foot.
The dress-suited cat asks if you're deaf.
Yes, if she chooses.
The angel's side-boy dissects red globules,
skinless, she works in leather.
Dr. Goldpate taps a scapular
with a metal meta-carpel.
The half-suited wydah with anticipated pin-tail
displays his vermilion beak.
The paranoid angel claims the ticking

switch-box will explode,
and the fridge jitters in anguish.
The postulant monk slits his throat in
deference to his toothache.
Salvador's Anthony repels temptation's horse
with ferocious thrust of the cross.
The surgeon muffles his breath
– only his eyes can be seen –
unmasks the heart of his myth.
I wake to a stapled skull, a scalp
unfeeling as weather-beaten leather.

The Green and Yellow Snake at the Door

I lift my head, expose my golden throat.
You marvel how I slither without legs,
that blood flows in my coiled foot.
I turn the pages of wisdom,
tilting my head,
yearning for admiration.

As the black cat glides past the window,
I feel air on my tongue, my earth-brown lips.
Search the mythology of
why.

Feathers clutched between my teeth,
I taste the bird-shrieks through my limb,
and learn the iron of my blue scales.
But never why.

I fly when the moon is dark,
bless the birds with eyes to light them in the night.

The punctured sky wraps me in its cold.

Bastet

In the beginning,
the Word became
toy to The Cat –

she is the beginning –
though not indifferent to God.

Words colour her palate,
her throat and lips
tease them to stutter,
flow into glossaries,
tongue their syllables
and inflame a taste
for capture and a stomach
for digestion.

They crawl the short tract of the verbivore,
smoulder and metamorphose
from cartilaginous apple
to flexible clay,
pounded and kneaded for expulsion
and writing in the image
of The Cat.

When wind brings a dance

the sparrows sway bodies, keep level heads,
and ancient coiled stems, camouflaged in
grey and green, shiver joy.

Knots and bark in shadowed cavities,
the cicatrice of fallen leaf, grant ambush points
for small black spiders.

Breasting a river of sunlight, overhung,
hover-flies swing,
hold their silver spots, feint, sashay, then –
a sudden dog-fight,
break,
come back to shift and hang.

In foliage depths and shallows,
vaults where weavers
topple hanging feeders,
claw bread against a branch and peck,

the black-masked bishop arrives.

Butter-thieves

jink and link
in mid-flight multitudes –
this autumn, their spring.

This heaven, my winter –
the butter-witch harvests hair,
twists my shape,
sticks her scissors in my back.
I'm her dolly – she turns the blades
to plunge again, snip one hair,
lets the rest vibrate –
follicled eggs
in clustered hibernation.

Spring wakens
to the soft green gnash of tiny teeth,
leads them into summer's fat pupation –
slumber of rebirth.

The moon skull turns away
as beloved earth tilts a haunch,
offers the dark hairy warmth of her kiss,
the carrion comfort of her gentle weight
to each fresh particle of my ash.

They split their mummied casks,
spread wings and sip their gins,
hesitate on leaves
for extraordinary moments –
join and fall.

Paradise

seeks the Isaiah future, the Genesis past,
confides the enlightened cat,
never the present.

He releases the dragonfly trapped behind his glass.
A moment? How long is a moment?
The crumpled wing, silver and veined.

It has a beginning and end.
It touches nothing before nor after future flicks to past –
into the garden and dart your wings,
dip your tail in the bird-bath.

If the present were all at once peacocks and spiders,
milking and bearded nipples, vassalage and cufflinks –
that would be Paradise unmaimed.

From the fishnet hammock, his tail tickles the grass.
If I were the china cat, he dreams,
I'd sleep in eternal now on the mantelpiece.
But this western alley-cat
craves the present among the fish ribs of past and future –
Addiction! Fairytales! Frantic action!

The micro-icicles that began with a bang
– and still exist –
have no necessity,
contingent because they began
and will melt.

He stretches a hind-leg skyward,
rocks the hammock.
And mind? Has mind another taste,
unsmuttied – that illuminates the drainage of
future into past?

Snare

The string is still,
the bow moves,
harmony showers the air.

But all is in my head,
and you remain outside.
Are you still? I move.
Do we become one song?

And dare I
snare my care?

Rose-fingered dawn
trembles our landscape,
washes my reverence –
sings my adoration of
bones and flesh
paradigmed in you.

Sappho's Rage

She stirs her glowing embers,
blows aside the mist on cliffs,
undarkens hidden clefts
and seeks blue forest deeps.

Her touches open me;
she steals down creepways never stole before,
seeks blue forest deeps
and rests on pillow slopes.

She plunders stealthways never crept till now;
I stretch my tendons to her flame,
take her deep inside my bushed-in cave
where lip on lip and tongue to tongue we burn.

We quench our fire in speaking streams
and spread our limbs on lacertilian stone.

Dune Wank

When pubic boys dune wank in some wild place,
and open each to each the others' sight,
their happy tulip touch grants each his grace.

They dance beneath the purple sky's sweet face –
they wing their wishes to the seagull's flight,
when pubic boys dune wank in some wild place.

They trip and skip along the sea's foam lace
and, tumbling in the ocean's chilling bite,
their happy tulip touch grants each his grace.

They leap and run, time's thieving to outpace,
then understand the fruitlessness of flight,
when pubic boys dune wank in some wild place.

Then sprawling unconstrained in sun's embrace,
they mark in sand the measure of their might.
Their happy tulip touch grants each his grace.

In silent circle standing face to face,
they welcome in the promises of night,
when pubic boys dune wank in this wild place
and happy tulip touch grants each his grace.

Original Sin

We're punished for the sin of fabled pair.
Men dreamed these stories of their carnal shame.
In fruity garden, wearing only hair,
they plucked the apple tree in their lust's game.

This disobedience – a prime offence –
earned them a frightful sentencing to death.
Expelled from garden, they were driven hence
to wilderness and slowly fading breath.

Their offspring, too, endured this punishment.
They had not sinned, yet treated were the same.
God's judgement was obscene, just excrement!
But we can now acquit our God of blame –

in our image, we made this God of tin,
so we, not God, are guilty of God's sin.

The Apple Tree's Prayer

I beg you, drench my thirsting root with rain,
present me with the windfall feast of life
and let me feel your joy but not your pain.

And let me drink your pleasure without bane,
enjoy life's happy dance, its flute and fife.
I beg you, drench my thirsting root with rain.

And I will never sumptuous earth disdain
nor ever swing the axe or plunge the knife,
so let me feel your joy, undo your pain.

The moon's dark smile and frozen face may wane.
If violation, bloody war be rife,
I beg you, drench my thirsting root with rain.

A harmless diet ours of fruit and grain,
the pleasure of sweet love with child and wife,
oh, let me feel your joy, undo your pain.

Then come, let's crow with pride, and without stain
embrace our neighbour, end our futile strife.
I beg you, drench my thirsting root with rain
and let me feel your joy, undo our pain.

What is this bondage

to a piece of earth,
a plant that raises scarlet candles every year,
a rock that captures bowls of rain,
to fine wind-tossed bushes crowding my dwelling's deck,
hastening clouds
and the coarse cry of hadidah?

What is this bondage to the phalanx of eland
who march heads-down into the north-west storm,
pied crows in pairs
who negotiate gales and croak their missions across chasms
of air,
to tiny maculate prinias
who explore the undersides of leaves,
and bokmakierie
who bares his throat with a territorial call
from the telephone pole?

What is this bondage to the small unadorned sunbird
who flits between my rafters
questing amongst the dried brunsvigias,
trapped in my loft
and killed by the neighbour's cat?

I am embroidered in this cloth,
my cover, my garment, my shroud.

hermit

oak leaves break loose
sing separate songs

old ousted elands seek solitary paths
unfriend all

not a shoalfish trapped in stone
but a god in a shrine
ring your self

sweep the minefield of love
and tiptoe through it

Home

Small spiders find a living in my house,
descend from threads and open up debate –
they're friends to me unlike the local mouse
who gnaws at lace and generates my hate.
I contemplate the shipwreck of my life –
I have no need for groups and festive times;
the presence of myself and absent strife
grants peace to mice and opens up my rhymes.
One spider tracks the trails of small black flies;
she waits and captures them with ruthless skill,
then watches me at chores through small black eyes,
and when I sing, she marvels at my trill.

Mother Death Whispers

I'll wink him away
with the wing of a bat
or the swish of a ringed cat's tail.

I'll find him in the mist of his morning tea,
in parting mother lips to her small boy's cheek,
in grieving her swirl in the whorls of industry.

I'll filch the laughter of sea and cloud,
where the grey woollen sky stains his cheeks,
where cat stalks the sharp blue dragonfly's pause,
where flights and sittings sing the same song,

while he keeps tryst with earthbound friends,
in the grief of his love for these few –
in the mist
of this absurd exile.

Fleet

A squall of shiplets blossoms,
single, signal linked,
riding one tormented sea,
each bow wave, wake,
unique.

Each petal tiller turn,
each bloom selected, free,
open to the skirl of gulls
and washing by
the sea.

Acknowledgements and Permissions

I am grateful to the editors of *New Contrast* and *Stanzas* in which versions of some of these poems have previously appeared, namely:

'Hermit', 'Psychopath', 'Snow Lover' and 'Ulterior Motion' in *New Contrast,* and
'The Apple Tree's Prayer', 'Fleet' and 'Home' in *Stanzas.*

I am also deeply grateful to Hugh Hodge who, without being responsible for the consequence, taught me the craft of poetry.

Quotations have been used on page 1 from the following sources:

> *The soul unto itself*
> *Is an imperial friend –*
> *Or the most agonizing Spy*
> *An enemy could send.*

Emily Dickinson, 'The soul unto itself' in *Collected Poems of Emily Dickinson* (New York: Gramercy Books, 1982 (first published 1890))

*

> *Not, I'll not, carrion comfort, Despair, not feast on thee;*
> *Not untwist – slack they may be – these last strands of man*
> *In me ór, most weary, cry* I can no more. *I can;*

Gerard Manley Hopkins, 'Carrion Comfort' in *The Penguin Poets Series* (Harmondsworth, Middlesex: Penguin Books Ltd, 1953)

*

A man cannot live without a steady faith in something indestructible within him, though both the faith and the indestructible thing may remain permanently concealed from him...

Franz Kafka, 'Aphorism 50' in *The Zürau Aphorisms by Franz Kafka*, translated by Michael Hofmann (United Kingdom: Schocken, 2006 (first published 1931))

Oliver Findlay Price

Printed in the United States
By Bookmasters